Books by James Wright

TWO CITIZENS

James Wright

TWO CITIZENS

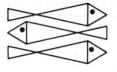
Farrar, Straus and Giroux

NEW YORK

Some of these poems first appeared in Chelsea,
Choice, Esquire, Harper's Magazine,
The Minnesota Review, Modern Poetry Studies,
The Nation, The New Republic,
The New Yorker ("Prayer to the Good Poet,"
"October Ghosts"), and Rapport.

For ANNIE, *my wife,*

and for RAE TUFTS,

our steadfast friend

Contents

"Well, bright boy," Max said, looking into the mirror, "why don't you say something?"

"What's it all about?"

"Hey, Al," Max called, "bright boy wants to know what it's all about."

"Why don't you tell him?" Al's voice came from the kitchen.

"What do you think it's all about?"

"I don't know."

"What do you think?"

Hemingway, "THE KILLERS"

TWO CITIZENS

Ars Poetica: Some Recent Criticism

I LOVED MY COUNTRY,
When I was a little boy.
Agnes is my aunt,
And she doesn't even know
If I love any thing
On this God's
Green little apple.

I have no idea why Uncle Sherman
Who is dead
Fell in with her.
He wasn't all that drunk.
He longed all life long
To open a package store,
And he never did anything,
But he fell in with Agnes.
She is no more to me
Than my mind is,
Which I bless. She was a homely woman
In the snow, alone.

Sherman sang bad,
But he could sing.
I too have fallen in
With a luminous woman.

There must be something.

The only bright thing
Agnes ever did
That I know of

Was to get hurt and angry.
When Sherman met my other uncle
Emerson Buchanan, who thinks he is not dead,

At the wedding of Agnes
Uncle Emerson smirked:
"What's the use buying a cow,
When you can get the milk free?"

She didn't weep.
She got mad.
Mad means something.
"You guys are makin' fun
Out of me."

2.

She stank.
Her house stank.
I went down to see Uncle Sherman
One evening.
I had a lonely furlough
Out of the army.
He must have been
One of the heroes
Of love, because he lay down
With my Aunt Agnes
Twice at least.
Listen, lay down there,
Even when she went crazy.
She wept two weeping daughters,
But she did not cry.

I think she was too lonely
To weep for herself.

3.

I gather my Aunt Agnes
Into my veins.
I could tell you,
If you have read this far,
That the nut house in Cambridge
Where Agnes is dying
Is no more Harvard
Than you could ever be.
And I want to gather you back to my Ohio.
You could understand Aunt Agnes,
Sick, her eyes blackened,
Her one love dead.

4.

Why do I care for her,
That slob,
So fat and stupid?
One afternoon,
At Aetnaville, Ohio,
A broken goat escaped
From a carnival,
One of the hooch dances
They used to hold
Down by my river.
Scrawny the goat panicked
Down Agnes's alley,

Which is my country,
If you haven't noticed,
America,
Which I loved when I was young.

5.

That goat ran down the alley,
And many boys giggled
While they tried to stone our fellow
Goat to death.
And my Aunt Agnes,
Who stank and lied,
Threw stones back at the boys
And gathered the goat,
Nuts as she was,
Into her sloppy arms.

6.

Reader,
We had a lovely language,
We would not listen.

I don't believe in your god.
I don't believe my Aunt Agnes is a saint.
I don't believe the little boys
Who stoned the poor
Son of a bitch goat
Are charming Tom Sawyers.

I don't believe in the goat either.

When I was a boy
I loved my country.

Ense petit placidam
Sub libertate quietem.

Hell, I ain't got nothing.
Ah, you bastards,

How I hate you.

Son of Judas

THE LAST TIME I prayed to escape from my body,
You threw me down into a tangle of roots.
Out of them I clambered up to the elbows
Of a sycamore tree, in Ohio, a place
I tried to visit.
I got within maybe a hundred and fifty yards
Of the strip mine.
I don't damn Mark Hanna or anyone else
In hell.
I have crawled along the edges of plenty
Of scars.
All I wanted to do
Was get out.

Now I've discovered my body that was alive
After all, I prayed to get back
Into my own.
I was perfectly willing to accept your world,
Where Mark Hanna and every other plant
Gatherer of the grain and gouging son
Of a God whonks his doodle in the
United States government of his hand.

Now, sure enough,
You came down and answered both my prayers.

I rose out of my body so high into
That sycamore tree that it became
The only tree that ever loved me.

And when I came back down into my own body
Some Hanna among the angels
Strip-mined it.

Now hovering between the dead sycamore,
That tree I made my secret love to,
And the edge of a wound I paid for by God,

I have bought your world.
I don't want it.
And I don't want all your money
I got sucked into making
Either.

I'm getting out, this time.
Out of that body I prayed to get out of,
Out of that soul that only existed
In the Jenny sycamore that is now the one wing,
The only wing.
It had little shadows of mark on it
That looked like feathers.
I never peeled off a single one.
You did.

Here's your money.
I didn't even count it.

Damn your own son,
And leave us go.

Prayer to the Good Poet

QUINTUS HORATIUS FLACCUS, my good secret,
Now my father, a good man in Ohio,
Lies alone in pain and I scarcely
Know where to turn now.

Fifty years he worked in that bitter factory.
He learned how to love what I found so ugly.
Ugliness. What is it? A bitter
Taste of one body.

Now, if I ask anything, I would ask you
How to gather my father to your bosom.
He knew, after all, how to love Italians.
Others said dagoes.

One good friend of mine, Bennie Capaletti,
Told me how in a basketball game, one person
Called him a dirty guinea, and Bennie
Did not even slug him.

Quintus Horatius Flaccus, my good secret,
Bennie Capaletti had the fastest
Hands in that fast Ohio Valley.
He could have killed him.

More than love, my father knew how to bear love,
One quick woman a dark river of labor.
He led me and my two good brothers
To gather and swim there.

I still love the fine beauty of his body.
He could pitch a very good Sunday baseball.

One afternoon he shifted to left hand
And struck out three men.

Every time I go back home to Ohio,
He sits down and tells me he loves Italians.
How can I tell you why he loves you,
Quintus Horatius?

I worked once in the factory that he worked in.
Now I work in that factory that you live in.
Some people think poetry is easy,
But you two didn't.

Easy, easy, I ask you, easy, easy.
Early, evening, by Tiber, by Ohio,
Give the gift to each lovely other.
I would be happy.

Now my son is another poet, fathers,
I can go on living. I was afraid once
Four loving fathers meeting together
Would be a cold day in hell.

Quintus Horatius Flaccus, my good father,
You were just the beginning, you quick and lonely
Metrical crystals of February.
It is just snow.

The Last Drunk

WHATEVER KILLS MY LIFE,
All that I have to lose
With a knife in my back,
It won't be booze.

You, you, if you read this,
I wouldn't have you think
I would give up the kiss
Of strong drink,

My secret root, my own
Jackhammer that blew off
The dead trees of my spine.
Hooch was enough.

For every body else
Who couldn't take what I
Can take through many hells
Before I die.

I sired a bitter son.
I have no daughter.
When I at last get done,
I will die by water.

She, what she might have been,
Her shoulder's secret gold,
Thin as her mother is thin.
I could have grown old!

THE TROUBLE WITH YOU IS
You think all I want to do
Is get you into bed
And make love with you.

And that's not true!

I was just trying to make friends.
All I wanted to do
Was get into bed
With you and make

Love with you.

Who was that little bird we saw towering upside down
This afternoon on that pine cone, on the edge of a cliff,
In the snow? Wasn't he charming? Yes, he was, now,
Now, now,
Just take it easy.

Aha!

The Young Good Man

THE YOUNG GOOD MAN walked out savoring
His own tongue instead of the lips
Of the wild crab apple.
You will believe this,

But there used to be places just on the other side
Of Cadiz, Ohio, where you could slip in
Without anybody knowing,
And find them sweet.

Everybody I knew, loved, and respected,
Like Charlie Duff, my cousin Dave,
George Ellis, Gene Turner from Bellaire
Who tackled me twice, and even I swear to Christ
John Shunk, the one man all the way from Pittsburgh
To Cincinnati who knew how to use
A diving suit and who got his name
In the newspapers all the time for
Dragging up the drowned boys,

Said leave them crab apples alone,
They taste so bitter you pucker
Two days at least. You bite one,
You'll be sorry.

2.

I don't know why,
One evening in August something illuminated my body
And I got sick of laying my cold
Hands on myself.
I lied to my family I was going for a walk uptown.

14

When I got to that hill,
Which now, I hear, Bluehart has sold to the Hanna
Strip Mine Company, it was no trouble at all to me.
Within fifteen yards of his charged fence I found me
A wild crab apple.

I licked it all over.
You are going to believe this.
It tasted sweet.

I know what would have happened to my tongue
If I had bitten. The people who love me
Are sure as hell no fools.

3.

You and I could not have been simple married lovers.
There are so many reasons I can't count them,
But here are some few:
You are much more intelligent and learned than I am.
I have a very quick felicity of tongue.
Sooner or later I would have bitten your heart
With some snide witty remark or other.
And you wouldn't stand for it.
Our lives being what we are,
We didn't have a chance.

I wish we had had.
I have written this poem to you before I die.
And I don't mean to die
For some good time yet.

1.

I WALKED WITH A BROWNED WOMAN in a time that grieved her,
The end of summer, above blue water, and the weeds
Came out wondering to her
About their names.

There was no one there to tell her in Serbo-Croatian
The name of that small flower song, and so we had to keep
Our own words in the vastness of that place,

And the dimness of mountains across the huge water,
And my grieving love wondering about being alone in the world,
And my love's clear face.

How could I tell her about their clear names?
I did not know them. I had to hold her.
That was all I had.

So I began. This one is the sun-blooded eye
Of a man who drifted weeping
Downhill into water, gathering, gathering

The awake woman. How are young lovers going
To take their way, and talk together?

Well,
For the first time in my life,
I shut up and listened.

2.

Those little birds ate singing
In a language that is strange to you and me.

16

So our love for them is a silly
Love, a sooth gathering and ringing
In a coil of snail shells.

The one thing that I most longed for to meet in the wildness
Here was a spider. I already know
My friends the spiders. They are mountains.
Every spider in America is the shadow
Of a beautiful woman.
Shy, marveling at the architecture
Of my own eyes, I found the best
Spider here. She spoke the best language.
And it spins her face.

3.

She wandered ahead of me, muttering to herself
That language of grief, the mountains and water that are always
A strange face, browned at the end of summer.
Ahead of me on the mountain path, my browned love told me clearly:
Come to me and love me clearly with the thinning shadow of the
        turtle.

I missed the turtle, the first time
I caught up with my love,
So we walked on.
Then we walked back. Oh, you should have seen her,
My love said to me, she was just going home
Between one road and another, and we don't even know
In Serbo-Croatian. What is your name,
I said.
I love you,
She said.

Ohio Valley Swains

THE GRANDDADDY LONGLEGS did twilight
And light.

Oh here comes Johnny Gumball.

Guido?
Bernoose got Lilly deVecchis.
Guido don't give a diddly damn.

Up on my side of the river
The cocksmen ramp loose.

The bad bastards are fishing.
They catch condoms.

What are you doing here, boy,
In cherry lane?

Leave her alone. I love her.

They knocked me down.

So I walked on up the river,
Outside the Jesus Jumpers' tent,

Oh God our help in ages past,
Our hope for years to come.

Here comes Johnny Gumball.

It took me many years to understand
Just what happened to her that evening.

18

I walked, stiff and lonely, up the long river.
The railroad dick asked me
Very politely what
I was doing there.

They're hurting a girl down there, I said.
Well, he said, you go on home,
And get out of this.

Johnny Gumball,
You and your gang caught up with my brother,
And beat him up. But that was no terror of mine.
My brother has his own life.

But I heard you and Guido cackling down below
That tent where the insane Jesus Jumpers
Spoke in their blind tongues,
And you laughed and laughed.

You thought that was funny, didn't you, to mock a girl?
I loved her only in my dreams,
But my dreams meant something
And so did she,
You son of a bitch,
And if I ever see you again, so help me in the sight of God,
I'll kill you.

I Wish I May Never Hear of the United States Again

THE RINGING and sagging of blue flowers,
And the spider shedding her diamond shadow down
On the turtle's body,
The old woman's hair lock golden spinning a web out of her clothes,
And the girls who have no trouble worrying
About the length of their dresses,
As they stroll slowly, vanishing into their own twilight
Beside the slim shoulders of the donkeys:

I can be silent among these.

One afternoon in northern California,
Which is a Jack London nut house,
I almost found my own country.
At the edge of a field
I gathered the neck of a buckskin into
My arms and whispered: Where were you
All this time?

Alone all this time, and bored with being alone,
I have been walking all afternoon at the edge
Of a town where the language is only to me
The music of mountain people.

In Yugoslavia I am learning the words
For greeting and goodbye.
Everything else is the language
Of the silent woman who walks beside me.

I want the mountains to be builded golden,
And my love wants the cathedrals to be builded
By time's love back to their gray, as the gray

Woman grows old, that gray woman who gave us
Some cheese and whispered her affectionate sound
To my love and me wandering silent in the breeze
Of a strange language, at home with each other.
Saying nothing, listening

To a new word for mountain, to a new
Word for cathedral, to a new word for
Cheese, to a word beyond words for
Cathedrals and homes.

The Old WPA Swimming Pool in Martins Ferry, Ohio

I AM ALMOST AFRAID to write down
This thing. I must have been,
Say, seven years old. That afternoon,
The families of the WPA had come out
To have a good time celebrating
A long gouge in the ground,
That the fierce husbands
Had filled with concrete.

We knew even then the Ohio
River was dying.
Most of the good men who lived along that shore
Wanted to be in love and give good love
To beautiful women, who weren't pretty,
And to small children like me who wondered,
What the hell is this?

When people don't have quite enough to eat
In August, and the river,
That is supposed to be some holiness,
Starts dying,

They swim in the earth. Uncle Sherman,
Uncle Willie, Uncle Emerson, and my father
Helped dig that hole in the ground.

I had seen by that time two or three
Holes in the ground,
And you know what they were.

But this one was not the usual, cheap
Economics, it was not the solitary

Scar on a poor man's face, that respectable
Hole in the ground you used to be able to buy
After you died for seventy-five dollars and
Your wages tached for six months by the Heslop
Brothers.

Brothers, dear God.

No, this hole was filled with water,
And suddenly I flung myself into the water.
All I had on was a jockstrap my brother stole
From a miserable football team.

Oh never mind, Jesus Christ, my father
And my uncles dug a hole in the ground,
No grave for once. It is going to be hard
For you to believe: when I rose from that water,

A little girl who belonged to somebody else,
A face thin and haunted appeared
Over my left shoulder, and whispered, Take care now,
Be patient, and live.

I have loved you all this time,
And didn't even know
I am alive.

Paul

PLENTY OF TIMES
I ran around in the streets in that small
Place. I didn't know what in hell
Was happening to me.

I had a pretty good idea
It was hell.
What else are you going to get
When you ain't got nothing?

You are going to get your friends who love paw-paws
Under a black street-light which will go damned if it blow.

You are going to wish you could be in love, and you are going
To die, and if you have anything in you that matters, you are going
To care for the man who picked you up on the street.

If I care for anything, I care
For the man who picked me up on the street.
Don't you remember? You said to me, Come on,
Get in, and we drove down to Brookside.

I remember your fury because I got a stuck piece of
Coal in my eye.

Come on, Paul, said your friend,
Rattling the tipple.
You told him to go to hell.
Because I had a speck of coal
In my eye.

You were making less than twenty dollars a week.
You drove that cracked truck down to Brookside lovelier and
   friendlier
Than Alcaeus loving Sappho.

You wouldn't even know what I'm talking about.

I wouldn't even know what you're talking about.

By God, I know this much:
When a fine young man is true to his true love
And can face out a fine deep shock on his jaw
(That scar so low off, that true scar of love),
And when a man can stand up in the middle of America
(That brutal and savage place whom I still love),

Never mind your harangues about religion.
Anybody could pick me up out of the street
Is good to me, I would like to be good

To you, too, good man.

In Memory of Charles Coffin

WHAT WAS THAT COLD AND UGLY THING
That snuck into your brain and killed
My love and your love. I would bring
The best of what I understand
In hand to you, were you alive.
I still care knowing you believe
In the body a soul can give.
You heard the soul rave and you send
A lonely echo of good Mars.
In that black summer when I worked
At the Mount Vernon, Ohio, Bridge
Company, I came damn near
Killing a man, and going blind.
All right, you said: Ben Jonson said
Give Salathiel Pavy one
More chance, and give yourself one more.
No, I have no idea where
You lie in Mary's ground alone.
I know, well, you would approve
Of this intricate sound I make.
It has three beats, though your heart break,

My loving teacher, whom I love,
It is almost too late to live.

ALL I AM DOING is walking here alone.
I am not among the English poets.
I am not even going to be among
The English poets after my death.
You loved them the best.
And you liked me, fine. It is still raining
This morning, this November morning.
And I am not even standing at your grave.
I am fiddling with a notebook in New York,
Wondering about Ohio where now at this moment
A leaf hangs on a locust thorn shredding
Its form into the rain.
John Keats, coughing his lungs out,
John Clare, crazy,
And Geoffrey Chaucer the only one.
And Edward Thomas, who got killed, the only
Soldier in this century who was sane.
If these lines get published, I will hear
From some God damned deaf moron who knows
Everything. The dead are nothing.
And he will be right.
The living giggle in the dark all night,
And the dead are nothing. I nearly got
My knees smashed at the Mount Vernon, Ohio, Bridge Company
That summer when I worked among the swinging girders,
To make enough money so I could write a good essay
For you. The essay wasn't all that good, but you loved it,
And you loved me. Steubenville,
Ohio, is a hell of a place to be buried.
But there are some lovely places to be buried.
Like Rome. Listen. So help me sweet leaping
Christ, it is going to be a cold day

In hell when any Johnny Bull knows
What I am saying to you:
I have found a woman who lives, and so
I am going to Rome with her
For a long time yet.
It is raining today in Steubenville.
Blessed be the dead whom the rain rains upon.
And damned the living who have their few days.
And blessed your thorned face,
Your shragged November,
Your leaf,
Lost.

AND SHE LOVED LOVING
So she woke and bloomed
And she rose.

And many men had been there
To drowse awake and go downstairs
Lonely for coffee and bread.

But she drowsed awake lonely
For coffee and bread.

And went upstairs
With me, and we had
Coffee and bread.

And then we were so happy to see the lovely
Mother who had been her mother a long time.

In this city broken on the wheel

We went back to the warm caterpillar of our hotel.

And the wings took.

Oh lovely place,

Oh tree.

We climbed into the branches
Of the lady's tree.

We birds sang.

And the lemon light flew out over the river.

The Streets Grow Young

1.

ONE FIRST SUMMER EVENING IN PARIS my love and I strolled among
The young students, studying the cathedrals
In one another's faces.
No rain there.
Inside an alley behind our own green bones
A peaked woman of fifty years, I guess,
Darted straight down at me in the darkness
And bluntly asked for a coin.

2.

A while later,
Hare Krishna, his cigar, his piano, and his orchestra
Forgave me for giving them cancer.

3.

The shrewd angel, the abandoner of his own solitude,
The native country of his hand,
Clambering from pit to scar up his mother's
Dugless chest. He has no woman,
But he has found how
To make a good thing out of hell.
No moss grows on those horny wings,
Even in Paris.

While he was forgiving me, the skinny whore staggered past,
Gnawing her spit-soggy
Claw of bread.

Okay. I accept your forgiveness.
I started the Reichstag fire.

I invented the ball-point pen.
I ate the British governor of Rhodesia.

(But that was a long time ago,
And I thought he was assorted fruits and chicken sauce.
Still, all the same.)

Okay now, hit the road, and leave me
And my girl alone.

4.

The amused Parisians snickered
While a retarded fat man on the corner
Shook a rubber rat in the faces
Of passing women.
The poor bastard needs money to die with,
And he can't even beg.

The Old Man Said Tomorrow

WHEN WE COME BACK to these
      black currants
And roses reeling heavily,
      blearily over
The green cress of rain,

He will be gone.

We will have to go all the way back
To Chartres, where he reels
      lightly, scarcely
Able to keep his wings folded,

As he rises into the honey stone that
      gathers
The gray rain of evening.

How can he keep wing with one
      flittering swallow?
When we come back, love,

He will be gone.

St. Benoît-sur-Loire

THE WHOLE CITY
Is stone, even
Where stone
Doesn't belong.
What is that old
Man's public face
Doing sorrowing,
Secretly a little,
A little above and
A little back from
A limp arm?
What is that stone
Doing sorrowing
Where stone
Doesn't belong?

The Old Dog in the Ruins of the Graves at Arles

I HAVE HEARD TELL SOMEWHERE,
Or read, I forget which,
That animals tumble along in a forever,
A little dream, a quick longing
For every fine haunch that passes,
As the young bitches glitter in their own light.

I find their freedom from lonely wisdom
Hard to believe.
No matter the brief skull fails to contain,
The old bones know something.

Almost indistinguishable from the dust,
They seek shadow, they limp among the tombs.
One stray mutt, long since out of patience,
Rises up, as the sunlight happens to strike,
And snaps at his right foreleg.

When the hurrying shadow returns
He lies down in peace again,
Between the still perfectly formed sarcophagi
That have been empty of Romans or anybody
Longer than anybody remembers.
Graves last longer than men. Nobody can tell me
The old dogs don't know.

Voices Between Waking and Sleeping in the Mountains

ALL AFTERNOON you went walking,
Just you, all alone,
And what you went wondering about
I still don't know.

I was trying to find something in that mountain snow,
And I couldn't find it by walking,
So I lay asleep
For three good hours.
There is something in you that is able to discover the crystal.
Somewhere in me there is a crystal that I cannot find
Alone, the wing that I used to think was a poor
Blindness I had to live with with the dead.

But it was not that I was dying when I went asleep
When you walked into the snow.
There was something I was trying to find
In that dream. When I finally fought my way
Down to the bottom of the stairs
I got trapped, I kept yelling
Help, help, the savage woman
With two heads loaded me, the one
Face broken and savage, the other,
The face dead.

Two hands gathered my two.

And you sang: Why, what have you been dreaming?

I don't know, I said.
Where were you?

You said you just took a walk.

Annie, it has taken me a long time to live.
And to take a long time to live is to take a long time
To understand that your life is your own life.
What you found on that long rise of mountain in the snow
Is your secret. But I can tell you at last:

There used to be a sycamore just
Outside Martins Ferry,
Where I used to go.
I had no friends there.
Maybe the tree was no woman,
But when I sat there, I gathered
That branch into my arms.
It was the first time I ever rose.

If only I knew how to tell you.
Some day I may know how.

Meantime your hand gathered me awake
Out of my good dream, and I pray to gather
My hands into your hands in your good dream.

What did you find in your long wandering in the snow?
I love your secret. By God I will never violate the wings
Of the snow you found rising in the wind.
Give them, keep them, love.

IN THE MIDDLE OF MY AGE I walked down
Toward a cold bloom.
I don't give a damn if you care,
But it half-rhymes with blossom.
And no body was ever so kind to me
As one woman, and begins spring
In the secret of winter, and that is why

I love you best.

I have a pretty good idea you won't believe
In your life. I don't deny our life is lost.
By God I want to live, and so do you.
I was too much a small boy to love
The cold trees you know.

Forgive and gather
My man's broken arms
Beneath them. This evening
The ice in New York City is bleeding.
What warms you?
What gathers beneath the cold wing, the west
Shoulder of heaven?

What is going to happen when we both die?

I love you best.

Bologna: A Poem about Gold

GIVE ME THIS TIME, my first and severe
Italian, a poem about gold,
The left corners of eyes, and the heavy
Night of the locomotives that brought me here,
And the heavy wine in the old green body,
The glass that so many have drunk from.
I have brought my bottle back home every day
To the cool cave, and come forth
Golden on the left corner
Of a cathedral's wing:

White wine of Bologna,
And the knowing golden shadows
At the left corners of Mary Magdalene's eyes,
While St. Cecilia stands
Smirking in the center of a blank wall,
The saint letting her silly pipes wilt down,
Adoring
Herself, while the lowly and richest of all women eyes
Me the beholder, with a knowing sympathy, her love
For the golden body of the earth, she knows me,
Her halo faintly askew,
And no despair in her gold
That drags thrones down
And then makes them pay for it.

Oh,
She may look sorry to Cecilia
And
The right-hand saint on the tree,
But
She didn't look sorry to Raphael,

And
I bet she didn't look sorry to Jesus,
And
She doesn't look sorry to me.
(Who would?)
She doesn't look sorry to me.

She looks like only the heavy deep gold
That drags thrones down
All day long on the vine.
Mary in Bologna, sunlight I gathered all morning
And pressed in my hands all afternoon
And drank all day with my golden-breasted

Love in my arms.

A Poem of Towers

I AM BECOMING ONE
Of the old men.
I wonder about them,
And how they became
So happy. Tonight
The trees in the Carl Schurz
Park by the East River
Had no need of electricity
To light their boughs, for the moon
And my love were enough.
More than enough the garbage
Scow plunging, the front hoof
Of a mule gone so wild through the water,
No need to flee. Who pities
You tonight, white-haired
Lu Yu? Wise and foolish
Both are gone, and my love
Leans on my shoulder precise
As the flute notes
Of the snow, with songs
And poems scattered
Over Shu, over the East River
That loves them and drowns them.

To You, Out There (Mars? Jupiter?)

I BELIEVE I CAN APPRECIATE the nobility of your dreams.
Some first thing, perhaps
Floating softly out of the dewrise of sulphur
Astonished to find yourself awake, life
Floating delightedly, flimsy to be so sudden
Between the one hand of a sard mountain
And the other locked sea-light of two chalcedony moons.

And then,
After the thousands, the years of gazing,
Fondling through lenses the tiny
Charming blue smoke-haze, spinning, a secret
Beyond all the moons.
It must look lovely,
So far off.
I wonder what you call it.

Look there! Look there!
Shift your great lenses aside slightly.
They are not all dining dreamily over minced hirsute puppy
And *moo moo gai pan.*
They are not forever drifting lazily in a cool evening across
Those turquoise niplets of shores, those cerulean
Inlets forever clustered with just the right number
Of clever and handsome black creatures
Who love to serve them.

No.
Shift your lenses aside a little,
Look there. Look there.

They are standing for hours in a line, huddling

Alone in the griped cold, hopelessly longing
To pray to someone whose name
Is Streisand.
They are smiling underground in the evening, storing
Long exquisitely sharp blades so that soon
They may touch each other's bodies.
They are sneaking aside to finger little bones
Which they call money.
They are carefully selecting their children, to slit open
Their pubes and inner arms.

To you out there,
Oh no, oh no, don't look here.
Sure, you will find a great plenty of things
On this tiny smoke-haze.
You will not find God.

RADIANT SILENCE IN FIESOLE
And the long climb up a hill which is only one feather
Of the sky, and to set out within the sky,
As the dark happy Florentine would surely gather
All that he had to gather and every night set forth
And enter the pearl.

Florence below our hands, the city that yielded
Up the last secret of Hell.
Fiesole below me and around me and the wings
Of the invisible musician Brother Esposito folded
Around me and my girl.

And the organ
Silent in its longing for the only love.
And Bach and Dante meeting and praying
Before the music began.

And a little bell ringing halfway down the hill.

And me there a long way from the cold dream of Hell.
Me, there, alone, at last,
At last with the dust of my dust,
As far away as I will ever get from dying,
And the two great poets of God in the silence
Meeting together.

And Esposito the organist waiting to begin.
And the little bell halfway down delicately drifting off.

And Florence down there darkening, waiting to begin.

43

And me there alone at last with my only love,
Waiting to begin.

Whoever you are, ambling past my grave,
My name worn thin as the shawl of the lovely hill town
Fiesole, the radiance and silence of the sky,
Listen to me:

Though love can be scarcely imaginable Hell,
By God, it is not a lie.

Names Scarred at the Entrance to Chartres

To Marsh and his music

P. DOLAN AND A. DOYLE
Have scrawled their names here.
You other stupid angels,
They have no wings
Here. Here all they have
Are squalling babies and the leaves
Of the wild strawberries you can still gather
Beside wet roads.

The cracked song
Of my own body limps into the body
Of this living place. I have nobody
To go in with
But my love who is a woman,
And my crude dead, my sea,
My sea, my sepulcher, the crude
Rhythm of my time.

This cracking blossom is my second America.
And though my first
Shatters itself cold with hatred, though
I might have given my leaves here
A long time ago,

P. Dolan and A. Doyle are the faint names
I enter with.

We have no home in the local strawberry leaves,
The wild peas' reverence, the living faces of men.

I have no way to go in
Except only
In the company of two vulgars,
Furies too dumb to remember
Death, our bodies' mother, whose genius it is
To remember our death on the wet
Roads of Chartres, America, and to forget
Our names. The wild strawberry leaf
Does not need to bother with remembering
Its own name, and Doyle, Dolan, and me.

All three Americans, drunk on our lonely women.

In our own way we hewed the town mayor
Among the several damned.
We sat up all night,
Rocking some frail accident of love who became
A secret of blossoms we had no business
To understand, only to remember.
Nameless builder of strawberry leaves,
So true to me in my lonely praying, so common
To the French builders who sing among lettuce
And proud tongue singing the clearest
Stone song.

God, I don't know who sat up all one night
Wishing in the name of sweet leaping Christ
He could get the kid to sleep before first light,
So he could get a couple hours to lie half-waking
And gathering the wild strawberry leaves,

That true woman.

I remember her name, but I won't tell.
I remember the names of Doyle and Dolan,
Who had their own ugly way to hack
Their names on this prayer.

These hideous wanderers hate life, they
Love, sullen, bitter, sitting
Up all night, waking beside women, waking
With leaves in their hands.

Who built this place?

Emerson Buchanan

EMERSON BUCHANAN, gun on his arm.
Uncle Willy the lone, Shorty the drunk.
All I wanted to do. That was the wrong
Place to be dead. All that we have,
Death, is Ohio. Franklin Pierce will scan.
Nobody else will scan, Allen the love,
Allen the lovely song, these are my friends.
Reader, alone, die. Die in the cold.
Publius Vergilius Maro scans.

Emerson talked too much. One time
On Christmas Eve I yelled out that he should keep
His mouth shut.

Shorty is dead, mewling,
Shorty is puke in the ground.
Uncle Willy is following
Two dead women out of sound,
Franklin Pierce was a single friend.
Once Nathaniel Hawthorne died with him.

Emerson Buchanan, who talked too much,
Shut up, and now he is one half-hendecasyllabic,

And almost an amphibrach.

I try and try to hear them, and all I get

Is a blind dial tone.

A SNAIL on Max Jacob's grave
At Fleury-sur-Loire.

A tiny whorl of colors,
Black and pale bronze.

Little whorls toiling out of
The poet's right toe.

I was in love with a girl who found
This grave for me.

We placed some wild morning-glories over
The sun-warmed granite of the poet's forehead.

We stood for a long time, watching
Rain fall straight down on the western horizon.

I love this poet, and I could not have found him
Without the girl whom I love. Too late be damned.

The snail beneath the right foot,
The toe pointing toward thunderclouds.

My right hand forgot Jerusalem,
And I forgot my cunning.

The snail remembered the Jerusalem of the Loire
And I knelt with my hat off.

The creature began the spinning path of his long journey,
While the bronze Jew snail of the rain bloomed.

We walked, holding hands, coil within coil, both looking
For love Max Jacob in the rain. We found him. We found our hands.

The sun came out long enough,
And too late be damned.

You and I Saw Hawks Exchanging the Prey

THEY DID THE DEED OF DARKNESS
In their own mid-light.

He plucked a gray field mouse
Suddenly in the wind.

The small dead fly alive
Helplessly in his beak,

His cold pride, helpless.
All she receives is life.

They are terrified. They touch.
Life is too much.

She flies away sorrowing.
Sorrowing, she goes alone.

Then her small falcon, gone,
Will not rise here again.

Smaller than she, he goes
Claw beneath claw beneath
Needles and leaning boughs,

While she, the lovelier
Of these brief differing two,
Floats away sorrowing,

Tall as my love for you,

And almost lonelier.

Delighted in the delighting,
I love you in mid-air,
I love myself the ground.

The great wings sing nothing
Lightly. Lightly fall.

Well, What Are You Going to Do?

I TOOK A NAP one afternoon in Ohio
At the end of a pasture,
Just at the good moment when Pet our poor lovely
Lay moaning and gave birth to Marian my calf.

What was I going to do? All I could do
Was wake and stand there.
I don't know anything about the problem
Of beautiful women.
I was afraid to run two hundred yards
To call my mother
And ask her what to do
With a beautiful woman.
Besides, she wouldn't know either.

Two hours.
Two whole hours.
While Pet lay mumbling among the Grimes Golden apples
That fell from time to time.
I ate two or three, maybe.
What was I supposed to do there
But eat the apples while Marian's face
Peeked out slowly?

I ate the apples,
And when Marian was born
I helped her come out.
I had been in love with a lot of girls, but that was my first time
To clasp the woman beneath her chin
And whisper, Come out to me,
Come on, come on, and you can be Marian.

I led Marian out of her mother's belly
Down in the cold
Autumn thorns,
And there was a pile of horse manure
I couldn't evade, and so by God
I did not even try.
All I could do was fall
From time to time.
Marian's face was all right, speckled with rust
And more white than snow.
The one I was the more in love with
Was Pet, the exhausted.

I lay down beside her, she snuffled, she smelled like a Grimes
Golden apple.
Then I carried Marian two hundred yards down the pasture.
She delicately sprayed the insides of her beginning body
All over my work shirt.

I don't know that I belonged
In that beautiful place. But
What are you going to do? Be kind? Kill?
Die?

October Ghosts

Jenny cold, Jenny darkness,
They are coming back again.
We came so early,
But now we are shoveled down
The long slide.
We carry a blackened crocus
In either hand.

I will walk with you and Callimachus
Into the gorges
Of Ohio, where the miners
Are dead with us.

They carry one another
In their arms, still alive.
What do I know of them? I know
Uncle Charlie prowling along the cold shores of their lives,
His meters broken,
And your voice the only living voice, the only
Wind the wind
Of this autumn.

I knew a beautiful woman when I was young.
She wept over me as one who could hardly care.
Diphtheria starred her earlobes,
And she wailed all night.
That time is gone when the young women died
Astounded to hear black veins in their bodies
Coil round one another all night.

Jenny, fat blossoming grandmother of the dead,
We were both young, and I nearly found you, young.

I could not find you. I prowled into my head,
The cold ghost of October that is my skull.
There is a god's plenty of lovers there,
The dead, the dying, and the beautiful.

But where are we,
Jenny darkness, Jenny cold?
Are we so old?
We came so early, we thought to stay so long.
But it is already midnight, and we are gone.
I have nothing at all against that song,
That minor bird I hear from the great frost,
My robin's song, the ancient nothingness.

Friends, I have stolen this line from Robinson,
From Jenny, and from springtime, and from bone,
And from the quick nuthatch, the blooming of wing upon the sky.

Now I know nothing, I can die alone.

She's Awake

My slim, high-strung
Beauty cannot sleep
On nights like this, and I wish I could follow
And soothe her where she goes.

I have an idea the road she walks on
Is a blue secret smoothed over
A long time now.

Wound after wound, I look for
The tree by the waters where
She lay somehow naked,
Somehow still alive.

Lying myself awake,
I imagine everything terrible in my own life,
The hitchhiking drunk, the shame of knowing
My self a fool.
Bad friend to me.

There was a mean kid I knocked down because I was weak.
There was a mongrel bitch I saw whose backside
Was set fire with kerosene and a firecracker.
I fought the son of a bitch who did it,
And I lost.

I bawled like an idiot
And crawled home, ashamed.

I try to imagine myself killing somebody,
My enemies the rats, the snakes, the
Drunk Indians, the
Bad men from the graveyard, hail,

They ruin everything, you give them a wing,
And they fly.

For God's sake, wake up, how in hell am I going to die?

It was easy.
All I had to do was delete the words lonely and shadow,
Dispose of the dactylic hexameters into amphibrachs

Gather your lovely life into my life,
And love your life.

To the Creature of the Creation

LONELY AS MY DESIRE IS,
I have no daughter.
I will not die by fire, I
Shall die by water.

Water is fire, the wand
Some body wandering near,
Limping to understand,
If only he somewhere

Could find that lonely thing
That fears him, yet comes out
To look through him and sing.

He cannot do without.

Without the moon, and me.
And who is she?
This poem frightens me
So secretly, so much,
It makes me hard to touch
Your body's secret places.
We are each other's faces.

No, I ain't much.
The one tongue I can write in
Is my Ohioan.
There, most people are poor.
I thought I could not stand it
To go home any more,
Yet I go home, every year,
To calm down my wild mother,
And talk long with my brother.

What have I got to do?
The sky is shattering,
The plain sky grows so blue.
Some day I have to die,
As everyone must do
Alone, alone, alone,
Peaceful as peaceful stone.
You are the earth's body.
I will die on the wing.
To me, you are everything
That matters, chickadee.
You live so much in me.
Chickadees sing in the snow.
I will die on the wing,
I love you so.